AGAINST ALL ODDS

Against All Odds

Hope, Peace, Resilience, Persistence, Determination, Love, Freedom

HERITIER RUDEHA

Harambee Development Initiative

ACKNOWLEDGMENT

To my dearest friends and family, thanks for being my cheerleaders and source of inspiration. I'm grateful for your constant encouragement, understanding, and support during the countless hours I spent writing. Your love and belief in me kept me going.

A heartfelt thanks to my mom for your love, wisdom, and guidance, Without you this book would not have been possible. I'm forever grateful. lastly, to all my professors and personal mentors, Your enthusiasm and belief in my work meant more to me than words can express.

Thank you all for standing by me every step of the way. your support and love have been the greatest gift I could ask for.

CONTENTS

$$\sim \text{I} \sim$$

Preface

In the vast tapestry of human existence, some stories transcend the boundaries of time and geography, weaving together threads of resilience, hope, and triumph. This collection of poems, entitled "Against All Odds," is a testament to one such extraordinary journey—a personal odyssey born from the crucible of a refugee's life.

Life itself can be a tempestuous sea, tossing us amidst its unforgiving waves. Yet, for those who have experienced the harrowing trials of displacement, the tempest becomes a tempest within, raging against the very core of one's being. It is in these depths that the true measure of the human spirit is revealed— the indomitable will to survive, to rise above the darkest of circumstances, and to reclaim a sense of belonging.

Within these verses, I invite you to embark on an intimate exploration of my own refugee experience—a chronicle of shattered homelands, shattered dreams, and shattered lives. For in sharing my story, I hope to illuminate the collective narrative of countless individuals who have faced similar adversities, who have known the anguish of leaving behind all that is familiar, and who have sought refuge in the embrace of unfamiliar lands.

Through the lens of poetry, I strive to capture the raw emotions, the fragments of memory, and the echoes of resilience that reverberate within the heart of every refugee. Each poem stands as a testament to the power of the human spirit—a testament to the strength that emerges when faced with the seemingly insurmountable.

This collection is not solely a chronicle of despair; it is a celebration of the human capacity to heal, adapt, and find solace in the beauty that can arise from the depths of suffering. It is a tribute to the countless acts of compassion, the outstretched hands of strangers, and the glimmers of hope that pierce through the darkness, lighting the path toward a brighter tomorrow.

As you immerse yourself in these verses, may you glimpse the intricate tapestry of my journey—a journey of resilience, growth, and transformation. May you find inspiration within these words and be reminded of the boundless strength that resides within each one of us.

For it is through the sharing of our stories, through the power of art and literature, that we bridge the divides between cultures, that we cultivate empathy, and that we pave the way for a world where no human is deemed "other." In turning these pages, you become a witness to the indomitable spirit of those who have defied the odds, who have risen above the challenges, and who have forged a path toward a brighter, more inclusive future.

Thank you for embarking on this poetic journey with me. May the verses within "Against All Odds" serve as a reminder that, even in the face of adversity, the human spirit can prevail, and that compassion and understanding can triumph over all obstacles that life throws our way.

~ II ~

~ III ~

LINE UP FOR SURVIVAL

1

Line up! Stand up! Never give up!
Look on, outlast.
Hold on, hold out.
Hung on, hold up.
Stand on, never give up!

Success is a zigzag line,
Not an overnight destination,
Every beginner is as limestone,
Passing through sublimation.
Race of ladies and gentlemen,
Men, women, and old women,
Competing to be hero and heroine,
Supermen and superwomen.

As fast as a deer running,
As high as birds flying.
Above the horizon, strive on trying,

While others stay on Amazon busy waiting.
Wiggling and wriggling as prodigies.
Wiggling and juggling to commit tragedies.

Many tragically gained comedy.
Others typically hum life-melody.
Nothing is impossible if you wish.
Everything can be possible if you push.

There are many obstacles, but don't crush them.
Continually historical, keep on the rush.
Behold! Many risks to take,
Countless sacrifices to make.
Call on! Be persistent, don't joke.
Dream big, with hard work, never forsake.

~ IV ~

THE JOURNEY BEGINS.

2

Surviving against all odds, they stand
Refugees have their fate in their own hands.
They have left behind all they ever knew.
To start anew and find a way through.

The struggle for survival is a daily grind.
Against poverty, against hate, against time
But they keep going, with strength and hope.
Their future is uncertain, but their spirit is unbroken.

For they know that they are not alone
That others have left their home.
And that together, they can make a way.
To a brighter future, and a better day

The long road ahead stretches everywhere.
For refugees, it is a journey that can't be denied.
They face the unknown with each passing day.

But they keep moving forward, come what may.

Their hearts heavy with memories of the past
But their eyes are fixed on a future that will last.
They travel through deserts, mountains, and seas.
With hope in their hearts, and dreams that will not
cease.

The struggle for survival is a test of will.
Against all odds, they continue uphill.
Their journey may be long, but their spirit is strong.
And they know that they will make it, no matter how
long.

For they are survivors, warriors of light.
Who refuses to give up, who refuses to lose sight?
Of the hope that burns within their hearts
And the love that never departs.

The long road ahead may be daunting and tough.
But for refugees, it's a journey of love.
A journey towards a future that is bright and free.
A journey towards a life that is meant to be.

So, they keep moving forward, step by step.
With courage and strength, and hearts that will not
forget.
That the struggle for survival is a call to rise
And to never give up, not until they reach the skies.

~ V ~

THE NEW LAND NEEDS AN EXTRA NEW HAND.

They are far away from home, from Congo to Kenya
They are very unfamiliar and strangers.
Refugees who struggled to adapt.
Their lives are forever changed.
Their broken memories shadowed their present.
Their future, undetermined and their past undermined,
Their lives are compromised just like an unclear distant
snapshot.

They face new challenges, every day.
The language, the customs, the food
But they persevere, come what may.
Their resilience, a testament to their fortitude

They learn to navigate this foreign place.
To build a new life, with every breath
Their hearts were filled with courage and grace.
Their future, bright despite the test

****

4

KAKUMA REFUGEE' CAMP

Welcome to Kakuma, a camp of refuge and pain.
Where the sun beats down on the endless plain
The people continue with strength and hope.
Despite the hardships, they learn to cope.

Forced to flee from their homes in fear.
Leaving behind all they held dear.
They arrived in Kakuma with nothing but dreams.
Hoping to find safety, or so it seems.

Yet years have passed, and still, they stay.
In this place where life is a constant fray
They long for a home, a place to belong.
Where they can sing their native song

But until then, they hold on to hope.
And find solace in the strength to cope.
In Kakuma, they have built a community.
A place of resilience and unity

And though they dream of a brighter tomorrow
Where they will find a place with no more sorrow
They know that until that day comes.

They'll keep persevering until their journey is done.

~ VI ~

THE LAND OF THE WARRIORS

5

The land full of dust and bare trees,
Promised of safety and freedom yet has none of that,
It's a cage where refugees seek respite from life.
Challenges warriors who stand tall, with heads held
high.
Their spirits are unbroken, though time passes by

For in this land, they have learned to fight.
Against the odds, with all their might
To protect their families, their homes, their dreams
To overcome the challenges, no matter how extreme

And though they long for a place to call their own
A sanctuary, where they can finally be.
They know that until that day arrives.
They will keep striving, for all their lives.

For in this abandoned land, they have become warriors
true.

Their spirit unbreakable, their strength anew
And though they hope for a brighter tomorrow
They know that in this land, they'll never lose their
glow.

ONLY THE STRONGEST
REMAINS STANDING

6

Only the Strongest remain Standing, true.
This is the mantra and motto that keep them through,
It's a place of endless rules.
Where getting anything requires standing in queues
The strongest only remain standing, day after day.
Surviving against all odds, no matter what happens.

For in this land, they have learned to be tough.
To stand their ground, no matter how rough
To weather storms and overcome fears.
To emerge victorious, despite the tears

And though they long for a place to call their own
Where they can rest and no longer feel alone
They know that until that day comes.
They will keep standing strong until their journey is
done.

For in this place, they've become resilient and brave.
With hearts that never falter, souls that never cave
And though they hope for a brighter tomorrow
They know that in this land, they will never lose their glow.

~ VIII ~

THE CAGE THAT SHAPES BOYS INTO MEN

7

It's all surrounded by barbed wire fence,
It's like putting their hands on fire, with no doubts they
face.
Giving in on this place of endless strife
Where boys must become men, just to survive.
The camp has been a teacher, harsh but true.
Of what it takes to make it through

For in this land, they have learned to be strong.
To face their fears, and never back down
To protect their families and stand their ground.
To become the men, that this land has found.

And though they long for a place to call home
Where they can rest, and no longer feel alone.
They know that until that day comes.
They'll keep striving until their journey is done.

For in these small huts, they have become warriors true.
Their spirit unbreakable, their strength anew
And though they hope for a brighter tomorrow
They still must go through and endure sorrow.

~ IX ~

BREAKING THE BARRIERS

7

It's all surrounded by barbed wire fence,
It's like putting their hands on fire, with no doubts they
face.
Giving in on this place of endless strife
Where boys must become men, just to survive.
The camp has been a teacher, harsh but true.
Of what it takes to make it through

For in this land, they have learned to be strong.
To face their fears, and never back down
To protect their families and stand their ground.
To become the men, that this land has found.

And though they long for a place to call home
Where they can rest, and no longer feel alone.
They know that until that day comes.
They'll keep striving until their journey is done.

For in these small huts, they have become warriors true.
Their spirit unbreakable, their strength anew
And though they hope for a brighter tomorrow
They still must go through and endure sorrow.

~ X ~

THE SCRAMBLE AND STRUGGLE FOR SURVIVAL

9

The struggle for survival is a battle cry.
For those who have suffered, and those who still try.
To find a way out of the darkness and pain
To a place where they can be free again

For refugees, the journey is long and hard.
Their spirits were assessed;
there were arts often scarred.
But they keep moving, one step at a time.
With hope as their compass, and faith as their guide

They have faced the worst that life can throw.
But they refuse to let their spirits go.
For they know that they are not alone
And that their struggle
for survival will bring them home

~ XI ~

THE VOICE OF EXPECTATION

10

Love and hope, a powerful pair
That can conquer all and take us there.
To a place where dreams come true
And the world is bright, and all is new.

During darkness, they shine brightly.
Guiding them through the coldest of nights
With love in their hearts and hope in their souls.
They could overcome any obstacle, any toll.

For love was the light that guided their way
And hope was the fuel that made them stay.
On the path that leads to a brighter tomorrow
Where joy and peace can cure all sorrow

~ XII ~

PINS ONE'S HOPE ON.

11

Hope sprung on them eternally, to face their despair.
For they sought it and were always there.
As a blue beacon of light, in the darkest of days.
And a true ray of sunshine, in the coldest of ways.

Aspiration was the fire that sang in their hearts.
Heal their open long-lasting wounds.
From the war that drafts their family and sets them
apart.
The Puff that causes them endless discords

But with aim and ambition, they rose above.
Found their strength again; to overcome.
The challenges that they faced each day.
Though, they got a life lesson, along the way.

~ XIII ~

SOLACE IN THE TIME OF HARDSHIP

12

In crowded camps and makeshift homes,
Refugees find solace where hardship roams.
Struggling to make ends meet,
Their resilience shines, a victory sweet.

Hustling in unfamiliar lands,
They build anew with humble hands.
In every obstacle, they find a way,
To keep their hope and dreams in sway.

Their struggles are a painful song,
But their spirits rise, resilient and strong.
Refugees, with hearts that yearn,
For a world where peace will return.

Refugees, like birds in flight,
Seeking refuge from the endless fight.

Through shattered cities and broken dreams,
They escape the horrors, or so it seems.

Hustling for survival, their spirits soar,
Building bridges where walls once bore.
Their struggles are etched upon their face,
Yet, hope and resilience leave no trace.

They carry stories of loss and despair,
But also, of strength and love to share.
Refugees, a testament to human will,
Their journey is a reminder to fulfill.

~ XIV ~

THE SHRED OF TENDERNESS

13

The tendency of tenderness knew no bounds.
It lifts them when they are feeling down.
Meanwhile, with more hopeless people all around
They attended weekly to the sick, and weak, without a
frown.

Discipline was the force that drove them on
And devotion was the light that made them strong.
Always held unto consistency, hoping could help them
conquer all.
Depends on family support to elevate them when they
fall.

For, during agony and hardship times
Hope and dreams became their lifelines.
Guiding them through the guidelines of the darkest days
Unto the dateline of the Red River's misty and myster-
ies; all the way.

Above the horizons, they shone, revived, and dived.
Across the black sea, they strove alive and survived.

****

14

The Light from Within

The light from within shone so bright like the morning
ray of hope, in the middle of the night.
It was a reminder that no matter how hard they fought.
Life would still always find its way to restart.

Destiny was the fire that fuels their souls.
Dreams were the trigger that made them whole.
Together, they use it to light their way.
And guided them through, to a brighter day.

For at a time of the toughest storm
Destiny and dreams would keep them warm.
And reminded them that they were never alone.
That God knew their suffering and was willing to give
them the crown.
If they could persevere a little long enough till they
gain.
For they knew for sure that they had to receive first
pain

Before they get ordained with the power to make life
their own

All these worked hand in hand.
Like a powerful force, helping them to stand.
In the strong hurricane of dust,
Gave them the courage to lift all their life's pounds.
And help them ascend from the evil of tombs.

$$\sim XV \sim$$

THE POWER OF UNCERTAINTY

15

They would hope for a guiding star.
To shine so bright, no matter how far
Looked for a crystal castle of hope,
They even desire to elope their life like an antelope.

For refugees, it was a source of strength.
Was also prompt and made them treated with contempt.
They were alone and helpless in their length.
Of struggle and pain, of loss and fear
That they had the power to persevere

Perseverance was an essential drive that kept them
going.
In all the times of hardship and the unknown
It was the glue that held them together.
Helped them in every condition and any weather.

Together with the power to endure the pain, they over-
came it.
Any challenge, any obstacle, any sum
And so, they found a way to a brighter tomorrow.
Where joy and peace could cure all sorrow.

THE WONDERWALL DESIRE.

16

The desire for joy and harmony among them was very
profound.
Therefore, they sang a harmonized song, humming for
their imaginary friend.
Hoping will lift them whenever they feel down.
With a hop and a skip, they would rise like the morning
crown.
The song gave them the urge, and willingness to give in
when all seemed lost.
The chorus of it carried the entire trip no matter the
cost.

For their wishes for peace and harmony were entwined.
An alarm, that the future is entitled to no one, and none
to define.
Neither by their circumstances nor their past should
they be judged.

But by the love they give and the hope of healing they
hold.

Was like an outstanding lamp that shone so bright.
The Alpha for the angel of light
Always giving flashbacks that no matter how hard
They could backslide, but they would still make it to the
summit.

With help and humanitarian aid, they could find a way.
To overcome all obstacles and any fray
They would build a future that is bright and free.
A future of peace, freedom, and possibility

~ XVII ~

THE AWAKENING SONG FROM FAR AWAY

17

The songs of freedom, burn so brightly.
A flame of activism rises and is displayed in every post.
It is a reminder that no matter how much the bleak.
Life can be, there's always a way to seek.

For refugees, the light within is a source of strength.
This is a reminder that they can go to any length.
To find a new home, a new start
And rebuild their lives, with love in their heart.

Love is the force that gives them hope.
That helps them cope and helps them grow.
It is the glue that holds them together.
And helps them weather, in any weather.

With love and light, they can rise above.
The challenges that they face, with courage and love.

And create a future that is bright and free.
A future of hope, love, and harmony.

~ XVIII ~

LOST AND ALONE

18

Lost and alone, with nowhere to go.
A child in search of a home
Their family and friends, long ago
Left behind, they roam.

The journey was long and filled with fear.
Through war and chaos, they fled.
The memories of home, still so near
But now they are filled with dread.

They cling to hope, day by day.
With each step, they fight to survive.
Their spirit is strong, they will not stray.
From the dream that keeps them alive

~ XIX ~

THE ORPHAN'S CRY

19

The orphan's cry echoes through the night.
As they face the world all alone
Without a family, without a light
Their heart, heavy as a stone

They long for love, for a warm embrace
For someone to call their own
But they soldier on, with strength and grace.
Their spirits never to be overthrown.

They find a way to make their mark.
To live a life, full of meaning and worth
Their journey, though often dark
Is filled with hope, and a sense of rebirth.

~ XX ~

ESCALATE ABOVE AND BEYOND.

20

In the face of adversity, they rise.
The single mothers, with determination in their eyes
Their journey is tough to endure.
But they hold on tight, with strength and courage to
ensure.

That they will not be defeated by the challenges they
face.
For they know that with perseverance, they can embrace.
A brighter future, one that is filled with hope.
leave behind the past, the pain, and the cope.

Their resilience is a testament to the human spirit.
For they rise above every obstacle and limit.
Their strength within is a force to be reckoned with
For they never give up on their dreams and their wish.

So, they keep moving forward, with their heads held
high.
For they know that with each step, they are one step
closer to the sky.
To a life filled with possibilities and joy
And leave behind the past, the sorrow and the ploy.

~ XXI ~

ONE FOR ONE, TOGETHER FOR GREAT IMPACTS!

21

Every man for himself, they know.
For there's strength within hustling together, which
helps them grow.
For in the face of foes and adversity, they remain strong.
And they keep moving forward, with their hopes and
dreams along.

Their resilience, a shining light in the dark
For they know that with each challenge, they will one
day disembark.
So, they decided to embark on a journey towards a
better tomorrow.
On the ship that was filled with joy, and free from
sorrow.

Their strength within is a force to be reckoned with
For they never give up, on their dreams to lift.

Themselves up, and those around them too
For they know that with hope, anything is possible to do.

They keep pushing forward, with their eyes on the prize.
For they know that with each step, they can rise.
Above the adversity, and the challenges they face.
And leave behind the pain, the struggle, and the dis-
grace.

~ XXII ~

THE AWAKENING DREAM

22

The hustle and bustle of a refugee young adult, never
give up.
For they know that with each challenge, they can
disrupt.
The adversity and the limits imposed.
And keep pushing forward, with their hopes disclosed.

Their perseverance, a shining example of strength
For they never give up, no matter the length.
Of the journey, or the road that is ahead.
For they know that with hope, they can be led.

To a life of possibilities and dreams come true
One that is filled with joy, and free with no glue.
A life of adventure, with skies bright and blue,
Where dreams become real, and hopes are renewed.

They would dream of endless opportunities anew,

Thinking of a new home full of wonder and magic cue
Where there will be freedom and the impossibility come
true,
Filled with boundless peace, liberty, and happiness, too.

They would dream of a world of wonder, where dreams
blossom and grow,
One without sorrows and free from the bruise.
With a heart full of hope and a spirit full of hue.
A life of abundance and fulfillment ensues.

~ XXIII ~

THE LONG ROAD, GROUNDED WITH REALITY.

23

The long road ahead was filled with rife.
A refugee's journey, wrought with pain.
They leave behind a former life.
Hoping for a chance to start again.

They face the unknown, with each step.
Their future is uncertain and unclear.
But they won't give up, they won't forget.
Their courage, unwavering and sincere

They hold onto the dream of a better life.
Of a world filled with hope and light
Their determination, a source of might
As they continue, through the darkest night.

~ XXIV ~

THE WEIGHT OF LOSS AND ANGUISH

24

Strength and resilience, their guiding light
Refugees and orphans, facing the fight.
Against adversity, they stand tall.
Their spirit is an inspiration to us all.

They face the world with courage and might.
Their struggles, a constant plight
But they never give up, they never falter.
Their hope is a flame that cannot be altered.

The road ahead may be long and tough.
But they keep going, with each step enough.
Their hearts are filled with love and grace.
Their determination, a steady pace

The weight of loss, heavy on their chest
Orphans and refugees, with a heart, distressed.

Their loved ones have been torn away from their embrace.
Their pain was etched on their faces.

The memories, still fresh and raw
Their dreams are shattered and flawed.
But they keep going, with each breath.
Their spirit, an unbreakable strength

The load of loss and distress is a burden hard to bear.
But they find a way, to rise above with care.
Their hope is a flame that cannot die.
Their love is a force that will never lie.

Hope and resilience, their unwavering power
Widows and orphans, with a heart, that towers
Above are the challenges that they face each day.
Their spirit is a beacon, which won't fade away.

~ XXV ~

THE MATCH TOWARD HEALING

25

The journey home, a distant dream
For refugees and orphans, on a path unforeseen
But they hold onto hope, with every step.
Their future is a dream they will not forget.

They long for a place to call their own.
Where their heart, can finally feel known.
A sanctuary, where they can finally rest.
Their spirit, finally at its best

The journey home may be long and tough.
But they keep going, with resilience and love.
Their spirit is a light that cannot fade.
Their hope is a force that cannot be swayed.

~ XXVI ~

COURAGE FOUND FROM WITHIN.

26

The strength within, a hidden gem
For refugees and orphans, on a dim path
Their spirit is a force that cannot be tamed.
Their hearts are a light that cannot be shamed.

They face the world, with an act of courage so bright.
Their struggles, a testament to their might
Their journey is filled with twists and turns.
But they keep going, with each lesson learned.

The strength within, a source of power so great
For refugees and orphans, on a path, that's not straight.
Their hope is a flame that cannot be dimmed.
Their spirit is a light that cannot be trimmed.

****

27

Education is the Key to the New World.

Then, why is education denied to the bastards?
Who is born out of marriage?
With no one to claim them as their dynasty.
Running out of courage,
Yet their mind is at war to stand fit,
Tired of trying to fit in while they were born to stand
out.

Poor children suffer a cruel fate.
They are just refugees seeking a better state,
Trying to start their life with a clean slate.
Their thirst for knowledge was left unquenched.
Their dreams were forever entrenched.

The classroom, a distant dream
For those whose lives are not what they seem.
Their future, a haze of uncertainty
Their potential is lost in obscurity.

But they fight on, with hope in sight.
Their thirst for knowledge, a guiding light
Their spirit, an unbreakable force
Their determination, a source of course

With free schools came free of knowledge

With only chalk and blackboards, the teachers taught.
No projectors or tablets, and no computers in the store
And internet access was something they sought.

With no scholarships or college, the future seemed
bleak.
For students who dreamed of a better life
In a class of 200, they struggled to speak.
And their education was filled with strikes.

Twenty thousand students, but only twelve teachers to
teach.
And each month, they were paid just fifty dollars.
The students sat on stones, with no desks in reach.
And their education is filled with hollers.

Mr. Bet, a discipline teacher, always with "Uncle Blue
sticks" in hand.
Brutally beat the latecomers and noisemakers too
For failing an algebra equation, they were banned.
And all day, they worked on the farm, feeling blue.

Despite the oddities, The Greenlight
secondary school was a place of despair.
But still, the students
persevered, with hope and care.

~ XXVII ~

THE CLINIC 7 HOSPITAL

28

The medical challenge, a daunting task
For refugees, disputing whose health is at risk.
Their access to care, a constant struggle
Their pain, an ever-present juggle

The hospitals, often far away
Their resources stretched every day.
But they soldier on, with strength and will.
Their hope, an unbreakable thrill

They persevere, with each breath they take.
Their health is a battle they must face.
Their spirit, an unyielding force
Their resilience, a source of course

In Kakuma and Kalobeyei, the refugees knew.
The click 7 luck of medication all too well.
With only two ambulances to serve more than a few

Their healthcare system was a tale to tell.

Chlorphenamine, well known as "piriton," was their
mainstay.
For their every sickness, no matter how dire
With no professional pharmacists, night, or day
The refugees' plight was like a burning fire.

No doctors to be found, no nurses to care.
People lay dying in hospital beds for weeks.
Others gave birth at home, in despair.
Their pleas for help, like a whisper that leaks
But no one came to their rescue or even dared.
When an ambulance was called,
or the police for aid.
They might come the next day, or so they said.

****

29

The Water Crisis

The water crisis is a daily plight.
For refugees, whose thirst is a fight.
Their access to clean water, a rarity
Their lives, a constant state of austerity

The streams, often dirty and unclean
Their thirst, a constant routine
But they keep going, with strength and grace.
Their hope is a light that will not be erased.

They find a way to survive each day.
Their thirst is a price they must pay.
Their spirit, an unwavering source
Their hope, a guiding force

****

30

The Food Ratio

The food ratio, a constant struggle
For refugees, whose hunger is juggling.
Their access to food, a scarce commodity
Their survival is a testament to their tenacity.

The meals, often small and meager
Their hunger, a constant trigger
But they persevere, with each bite they take.
Their hope is a light that will not shake.

They find a way to make ends meet.
Their hunger is a price they must beat.
Their spirit is a force that cannot be tamed.
Their hope is a light that cannot be maimed.

****

31

The Struggle for Basic Needs

The struggle for basic needs, a constant test
For refugees, whose lives are a quest.
Their access to education, medical care, clean water,
and food
Often blocked by bureaucracy and greed

Their survival is a fight they must lead.
Their potential is often left untapped.
Their dreams are forever capped.
But they keep striving, day after day.

Their resilience is a force that won't sway.
Their spirit, an unbreakable flame
Their hope is a light that will not be tamed.
for, they are also dreaming of walking into the Hall of
Fame,

~ XXVIII ~

CAMP MANAGER

32

Poor camp management, a cruel fate
For refugees, whose lives are at stake.
Their living conditions, often dire
Their basic needs are left to expire.

The shelters, often overcrowded and small
Their privacy is non-existent.
Their safety is a constant concern.
Their hope, a flame that's hard to burn.

But they keep fighting, with each day new.
Their resilience is a true force.
Their spirit, an unyielding power
Their hope, a force that won't cower.

****

33

The Turkana Tribe

The Turkana tribe had a cruel fate.
For refugees, whose lives they dictate.
Their hostility, a constant threat
Their safety is a risk they must take.

The attacks, often violent and fierce
Their fear, a constant pierce
Their hope is a light that's hard to see.
Their spirit is a free force.

But they keep holding, with each day's dawn.
Their resilience is a strong force.
Their spirit, an unbreakable shield
Their hope, a force that won't yield.

****

34

Makarao Brutality

Makarao is well known as a police officer on duty.
Famous for their brutality, a cruel fate

To refugees, whose lives they dictate.
Their rights were often trampled on.

Their dignity is forever gone.
The beatings, often severe and cruel
Their fear, a constant fuel
Their hope is a light that's hard to find.

Their spirit, a force that's kind.
But they keep standing, with each day's rise.
Their resilience is a force that won't compromise.
Their spirit, an unbreakable heart
Their hope is a force that won't depart.

****

35

The Sense of Belongings

The struggle for belongings, a daily grind
For refugees, whose possessions are hard to find.
Their homes, often far away
Their memories are lost in the fray.

The thefts, often rampant and bold
Their loss, a constant hold
Their hope is a light that's hard to see.
Their spirit is a force that will not depart.

They cling to hope, a lifeline in the dark
A spark that ignites their will to embark
On a journey towards a brighter tomorrow
Free from the pain, free from the sorrow

They dream of a place to call their own.
A place where they can thrive and be known.
Where they can start anew, with a clean slate.
And leave behind their past and their fate.

The struggle for belongings, a burden to bear
But their hope is a force that they will not spare.
For they know that with hope comes the chance.
To change their circumstances, advance

So, they hold on tight, to that glimmer of light.
And fight for their belongings, with all their might.
For they know that with each possession they reclaim
They inch closer to a life free from pain.

****

~ XXIX ~

CULTURE AND DIVERSITY.

36

Cultural differences can create hostility,
A war between Nuer and Dinka tribes tore families
apart,
Their language barriers exacerbate the animosity,
But the soccer football federation brought a glimmer of
hope to start.

Kakuma's soccer league, a place to come together and
play,
To compete and show their skills, to bond and make new
friends,
But the rivalry between teams also led to dismay,
Sometimes tearing the community apart until the game
ends.

A ball that once was a symbol of division and hate,
Became a tool for unity and peace within the refugee
camp,

A chance to set aside their differences and celebrate,
The power of sports to heal and unite, a shining lamp.

****

37

The Blossom of Savannah

Amidst the chaos and the strife
The refugee clings to hope for a better life.
A place where they can thrive and grow.
Where happiness and peace can flow

Their past, a distant memory
Their future, a chance to be free.
To leave behind the pain and sorrow
And start anew, with a brighter tomorrow.

They dream of a place without fear.
Without hunger, without tears
Where they can build a life of their own
And never again feel alone.

So, they hold on tight to their dreams.
For they know that with hope, anything it seems.
Is possible, and they can overcome it.
Any challenge that comes, until they reach their home.

~ XXX ~

THE BRIGHT FUTURE AHEAD

38

The refugee journey is long and hard.
But they hold on tight to their dreams, undeterred.
For they know that with each step they take
They inch closer to a brighter fate.

Their future, a blank canvas to paint
With bright colors of hope and joy, no more restraint
Their past, a lesson learned, a guide.
For the future, they seek, with open eyes.

They dream of a life with purpose and meaning.
Where their talents and skills can be gleaming
A place where they can contribute and give.
And live a life of dignity, and pride to live.

So, they press forward, with hope in their heart.
For they know that with perseverance, they can start.
A new life, a new beginning, with a bright future ahead
And leave behind the past, the pain and the dread.

****

39

The Greenland on the other side of the River

The refugee's journey is a tough one to endure.
But they hold on to their hopes, steadfast and pure.
For better resettlement, they strive.
Where they can thrive, and truly come alive.

They dream of a place that feels like home.
Where they can settle, and no longer roam.
A place where they feel welcomed and valued.
And where their dreams can finally be pursued

They hope for a life in which opportunities abound.
Where they can work, and their talents can be found.
A place where they can belong, and truly be seen.
And where their future can be bright and serene

So, they keep their hopes high, and their dreams alive.
For better resettlement, they will strive.
And with each step they take, they will come closer.
To a life they deserve, and a brighter future.

****

40

The Art of Letting Go

It takes time to finally stop relapsing on neverending
thoughts.
So, they adapt as time goes on, anticipating positive
results,
They let out that they needed persistence and persever-
ance,
To help them learn how to hold on tight.
Forgetting the broken memories of the past,
And grasp on the future promises, with no pain, and
strife
But as time went on, they realized the art.

Yes, the art of letting go and welcoming a fresh start.
For in their heart, they found strength.
To release the past and all length
To embrace the present, and what it brings
To spread their wings and begin to sing.

And though the scars of the past remain.
I know that they can overcome the pain.
For the art of letting go, they found.
The power and the path toward healing, and to truly
abound.

~ XXXI ~

FINDING PEACE OF MIND.

41

Why should one wish for money and wealth?
with no peace and precious gift of health?
Time is money, so says an adage.
Yet, they seem to be getting none of the average.

They are stuck in chaos, noise, and disease.
But as time went on, they discovered the way.
To find peace within, no matter the fray
For in their heart, they found calm.
That comes from within, like a healing balm.

They learned to breathe, let go, and trust.
believed in never giving up, no matter how tough.
Stayed focused on the journey ahead, no matter how
rough.
And though the future is still unknown.
They now know that they are not alone.

For in finding peace within, they found.
The strength to endure, and to truly abound.

****

.

42

The Power of Forgiveness

With punched life thrown their way, they learned to
hate.
I mean, to hate injustice, pain, and fate.
But as time went on, they discovered the way.
To forgive, and to truly live each day.

For in their heart, they found the power.
To let go of anger, and to flourish the flower.
They learned that forgiveness is not weak.
But the gateway to healing and truth-seeking.

And though the scars of the past remain.
They believe that they can overcome the pain.
For in the power of forgiveness, they found.
The key to healing, and to truly abound.

****

43

The Power of Resilience

Life is a Mary-go-around, passing the stick to the next in
line.
They had their fair and unfair share,
So marginal, adjusting as a water plant, with edges so
rare.
They faced and accepted the taste of it.

Most likely, the test unravels tenderness, strength, and
their best.
As time went on, they discovered the way.
To be resilient, and to truly stay.
For in their heart, they found strength.
To endure, to persist, and to truly length.

They learned that resilience is not just a skill.
But the essence of life, and the will to fulfill.
And though the journey ahead is still long.
They know that they can keep going strong.
For in the strength of resilience, they found.
The power to overcome sorrowful pang.

~ XXXII ~

FLYING ABOVE THE HORIZON

44

All eyes are on them, most of the world is on its knees,
The war going on from Rashia to Ukraine,
China and Taiwan
The Niger Government was overthrown,
M23 trying to take over Congo, and is overblown.
Israel fights with Pakistan, over what is called "desecra-
tion.
The world has become a War zone,
very unsafe for the new unborn.
they felt the weight.
Of the struggle, the pain, and the hate

But as time went on, the victims discovered the way.
To rise above, and to truly sway
For in their heart, they found the light.
To shine bright, and to take flight.

They learned that rising above is not just a dream.

But the reality of life, and the power to redeem.
And though the darkness may still surround.
They are hoping that they can truly astound.
For in rising above, they found.
The strength to conquer, and to truly abound.

~ XXXIII ~

THE OASIS IN THE MIDDLE OF
THE DESERT

45

They are thirsty and seeking an oasis in the desert,
they are wandering and lost,
seeking and searching for a way.
To escape the pain and fear of yesterday

The struggle for survival never ends.
For those who flee from their homes and friends
They face the obstacles with each step they take.
Their hearts heavy with sorrow and ache

They persevere through the toughest of times.
With hope as their guide, and faith in their minds
For refugees, the road is long and hard.
Their journey was marked by loss and scars.
But they keep moving, with strength and grace.
Determined to find a safer place.

****

46

The Gift of Gratitude

In the refugee camp, they felt the loss.
Of the comfort, the love, and the toss
But as time went on, they discovered the way.
To be grateful, and to truly stay

For in my heart, they found the gift.
Of gratitude, and to truly uplift
They learned that being grateful is not just a choice.
But the essence of life, and the power to rejoice.

And though the challenges may still arise.
They know that they can truly rise.
For in the gift of gratitude, they found.
The power to thrive, and to truly astound.

****

47

The Beauty of Equity.

Beauty is in the eye of the beholder, so they were told.
However, they felt alone, apparently unwanted.

In the sea of strangers,
and the basin lake trail of passengers.

Yet as time went on, they discovered the way.
To celebrate diversity, and to truly sway
For in Their heart, they found beauty.
Of diversity, and to truly see.

The path through which they could recover.
But the unclear sheer light of discovery,
Was still deemed blurred and blunt.
They therefore learned that inclusiveness is not just a
fact.
But the richness of life, and the power to impact.

And though the differences may remain.
They know that they can truly sustain.
For in the beauty of diversity, they found.
The power to unite, and to truly astound.

~ XXXIV ~

THE HOPE OF A NEW DAY

48

All alone, feeling sensations of dispersion and despair.
Of the uncertainty, the fear, and the tear
But as time went on, they discovered the way.
To hope for a new day, and to truly sway

For in their heart, they found hope.
Of a new day, and to truly cope.
They learned that hope is not just a wish.
But the strength to endure, and to truly relish.

And though the darkness may still loom.
They know that they can truly bloom.
For in the hope of a new day, they found.
The power to persevere, and to truly astound.

Their struggles are many, their hearts heavy,
But their spirits endure, remarkably steady.
In foreign lands, they strive and hustle,

Building lives anew, despite the tussle.

They labor with hope, their dreams unbroken,
For a brighter future, their hearts have spoken.
Though their journey has been rough,
They find strength in resilience, enough.

~ XXXV ~

THE HARD NUT

49

In the foreign lands far away from their own, Refugees find themselves alone.
Through war and strife, they've fled, Seeking shelter, a hopeful thread.
Leaving behind all they've ever known. Embracing around what is in their zone.
Through deserts and vast and treacherous seas, they seek solace, an end to unease.
Struggling through cold borders, putting their entire lives on hold,
The blue cloud is full of stories of resilience that are seldom told.
They are Hustling and bustling to find a hideout, a place to call home,
In the pending face of adversity and rejection to re-settlement.

Will all the ramble bubbles still bravely roam?

Their courage shines through the darkest night,
Their determination is a crystal beacon of light.
Drifting for refuge, massacres' hard nut of shattered trend,
They are survivors, the victims of the exploited land.
Keep on fighting for a future, where hope expands.

****

50

The New Dawn Finally Arrived

It was a battle of no return, the weight of struggle,
Pain and hate surrounded the unnamed soul,
With numerous unmarked graveyards
But as time went on, a discovery was made,
To rise above and truly sway, to a new goal.

For in their heart, the light was found,
To shine bright and take flight beyond the ground,
Learning that rising above is not just a dream,
But the reality of life, and the power to redeem.

And though the darkness may still surround,
The unnamed soul knows they can astound,
For in rising above, the strength was found,
To conquer and truly abound.

In the refugee camp, the loss was felt,

Of comfort, love, and the toss of fate that dealt,
But as time went on, a new path was paved,
To be grateful and truly stay, is a gift to be saved.

For in their heart, the gift was found,
Of gratitude, to uplift and astound,
Learning that being grateful is not just a choice,
But the essence of life, and the power to rejoice.

~ XXXVI ~

The End!

Author's Background:

Heritier, widely known as Joshua, was born in the Democratic Republic of Congo, a country rich in culture and history. However, his early years were marked by adversity as he found himself displaced from his homeland due to conflict. Joshua's journey led him to Kakuma Refugee Camp, a place that would shape his character and fuel his determination for a brighter future.

Life in Kakuma Refugee Camp:

Growing up in Kakuma Refugee Camp, Joshua experienced first-hand the challenges and resilience of refugee life. Despite the difficult circumstances, he found solace in books and discovered a passion for storytelling. Through the power of words, Joshua transcended the boundaries of his physical surroundings and embarked on a journey of self-discovery and personal growth.

The Harambee Development Initiative:

Driven by a deep sense of responsibility and a desire to make a positive impact, Joshua eventually founded the Harambee Development Initiative. This organization aimed to empower refugees and marginalized communities through education, skill development, and community-building initiatives. Joshua's vision and leadership transformed the lives of many, providing hope and opportunities for a better future.

Writing as a Medium for Change:

Motivated by his own experiences and the stories of those around him, Joshua turned to writing as a powerful medium for change. Through his book, he seeks to shed light on the challenges faced by refugees and amplify their voices, painting a vivid picture of resilience, determination, and the universal human spirit.

The Book's Purpose:

In this compelling book, Joshua weaves together his narrative, the stories of others, and his insights as a community leader. He invites readers on a journey of empathy, understanding, and inspiration.

Through his words, Joshua aims to challenge stereotypes, break down barriers, and ignite conversations that lead to positive social change.

Joshua's Message:

Joshua's message is one of hope, resilience, and the transformative power of education and community. His story serves as a testament to the strength of the human spirit and the ability to overcome adversity. With his book, Joshua aims to inspire readers to embrace compassion, advocate for social justice, and work towards a world where everyone has the opportunity to thrive.

As an author, Joshua brings a unique perspective shaped by his background, experiences, and dedication to creating a better world. His storytelling prowess and commitment to social change make him a voice worth listening to and a catalyst for inspiring action.